Other Books by John Bradley

POETRY
Everything in Motion, Everything at Rest (2020)
Spontaneous Mummification (2020)
Agitprop (2019)
Erotica Atomica (2017)
And Thereby Everything (2015)
Love-In-Idleness: The Poetry of Roberto Zingarello (2015)
One Day You a Mountain Shall Be: The Lost Poetry of Cheng Hui (2014)
You Don't Know What You Don't Know (2010)
Terrestrial Music (2006)
Add Musk Here (2002)
To Dance with Uranium (1995)
The New Wine Dreaming in the Vat (1993)
From the Faraway Nearby (1992)
Love-In-Idleness: The Poetry of Roberto Zingarello (1989)
All for Blanca (1988)
A-E-I-O-U (1981)

PROSE
Trancelumination (2011)
War on Words (2006)

ANTHOLOGIES
Eating the Pure Light: Homage to Thomas McGrath (2009)
Learning to Glow: A Nuclear Reader (2000)
Atomic Ghost: Poets Respond to the Nuclear Age (1995)

HOTEL MONTPARNASSE
Letters to César Vallejo

JOHN BRADLEY

DOS MADRES
2021

DOS MADRES PRESS INC.
P.O. Box 294, Loveland, Ohio 45140
www.dosmadres.com   editor@dosmadres.com

Dos Madres is dedicated to the belief that the small press is essential to the vitality of contemporary literature as a carrier of the new voice, as well as the older, sometimes forgotten voices of the past. And in an ever more virtual world, to the creation of fine books pleasing to the eye and hand.

Dos Madres is named in honor of Vera Murphy and Libbie Hughes, the "Dos Madres" whose contributions have made this press possible.

Dos Madres Press, Inc. is an Ohio Not For Profit Corporation and a 501 (c) (3) qualified public charity. Contributions are tax deductible.

Executive Editor: Robert J. Murphy

Illustration & Book Design: Elizabeth H. Murphy
www.illusionstudios.net

Typeset in Adobe Garamond Pro & Arcitectura
ISBN 978-1-953252-34-0
Library of Congress Control Number: 2021942873

First Edition
Copyright 2021 John Bradley
All rights reserved. No part of this book may be reproduced or transmitted in any form or by any means graphic, electronic or mechanical, including photocopying, recording, taping or by any information storage or retrieval system, without the permission in writing from the publisher.
Published by Dos Madres Press, Inc.

Acknowledgements

Inspector Georges Simenon, that most esteemed and exacting investigator for the Hotel Montparnasse, has discovered that the following documents have appeared in various publications, sometimes in altered form:

The Bitter Oleander: "One day you find under an iron tree a heel of bread," "The Art of Invisibility," and "The wind lives in a vase in the yellow house"

Calibanonline: "Into and Out of This World: An Interview with Cesar Vallejo's Death Mask" and "Paul Celan does not like to be touched"

Homage to Vallejo, ed. Christopher Buckley: "We Do Not Mourn You, Cesar Vallejo"

Many Mountains Moving: "In Other Violence Today"

Nonmaterialism Foundation: "Regarding the Diagram of a Bomb," "And the people made of ash would eat," and "When Poetry Is History's Fable"

Otoliths: "Yeah, Jean Cocteau and I"

The Room: "For Joyce Mansour, Lost in Cairo"

for Jana

Table of Contents

Residents of Hotel Montparnasse xi

PREFACE
[Dear Mr. Bradley], ...1

CHAPTER ONE
[What, then, did the earth tell you], ...5
[You checked into room number 39], ...6
[This note was found in the restaurant], ...8
[But tell me, my friend, how], ...9
[My Dear Monsieur Vallejo], ... 10
[Thou shalt not take the name], ... 12
[You're sure you want to do this], ... 14
[Date: September 10, 19 [Unreadable]], ... 15
[I was handed this today], ... 17
[A swastika found spray-painted], ... 19

CHAPTER TWO
[Dear César, you know what's coming], ... 23
[I can smell sulfur], ... 25
[*Don't forget what your hat and shoes*],. 26
[Yeah, Jean Cocteau and I], ... 28
[Would I like you to shave my legs], ... 30
[I've left the items you requested], ... 31
[Well, there's not a lot known], ... 33
[You tell the story again], ... 35
[Before there was red], ... 37
[Angel was polishing the leaves], ... 38

CHAPTER THREE

[Dear, Dearest César], ... 43
[Regarding the rumor of a diagram], ... 44
[When asked why he made origami], ... 46
[Because now they ~~fornicate~~ violate your mail], ... 48
[There was a line for tickets], ... 49
[I came across a faded book], ... 51
[You left the hotel *without official leave*], ... 52
[Compadre], ... 54
[Monsieur V], ... 56
[César, Gertrude Stein read this], ... 58

CHAPTER FOUR

[It's the solstice], ... 63
[Due to the sudden vowel shortage], ... 65
[That photo you sent], ... 66
[So sorry you had to wake], ... 67
[In Minsk, mercury leaks], ... 68
[That smoky scent], ... 69
[*Last night, I was in a tunnel*], ... 70
[Check your door, César], ... 72
[One day you find under an iron tree], ... 74
[The Paris light, César], ... 75

CHAPTER FIVE

[Say something], ... 79
[I know what happened], ... 81
[Your voice, César, spreads], ... 83
[*I'm traveling faster now*], ... 84
[You've shaved, César], ... 86
[The wind lives in a vase], ... 87

[And so this guy says to his friend], ... 88
[Here's my list of *Impossible Things*], ... 89
[Two pedestrians], ... 90
[I know you'll hate this], ... 92

CHAPTER SIX

[They're afraid of you], ... 97
[This was found on the floor], ... 98
[I know what you're doing, friend], ... 99
[Alma told me—forgive her, friend], ... 101
[Because the stars], ... 103
[A revolver with three bullets], ... 104
[Dear Mademoiselle Corday], ... 105
[Last night, when all the lights], ... 107
[Rain, tapping on my shoulder], ... 109
[Written in soap], ... 110

CHAPTER SEVEN

[No, César, I don't think you should], ... 113
[Later, after you were questioned], ... 115
[Because the eye doesn't want to hear], ... 117
[This time we were in a diner], ... 118
[Your ravenous heartbeat], ... 120
[At 4 a.m., I see you], ... 121
[Something for your digging], ... 122
[A votive candle on the radio], ... 123
[Don't tell, César], ... 125
[Thou shalt walk], ... 126

NOTES 129

APPENDIX

[Dear Reader], ...131
[Jeanette sent me this], ...133
[Found inside the rooftop pigeon coop], ...134
[Frida claims she found this], ...137
[Inside a coyote's stomach], ...139
[This so-called "interview"], ...140
[Found tucked into a copy of *Trilce*], ...144
[I remember. I can't remember], ...146
[This text, as well as the next], ...148
[Do not disturb], ...150
[And then, with my fingernail], ...152

NOTES 155

About the Author. 157

Residents of Hotel Montparnasse
(During the Period Vallejo Was a Guest)

Alma, chambermaid
Angel, hotel maintenance
Guillaume Apollinaire, electrician
Antonin Artaud, guest
Gaston Bachelard, director of mail services
Djuna Barnes, guest
Charles Baudelaire, guest
Brutus, feral cat
Miguel Carablanca, house doctor
Leonora Carrington, guest
Paul Celan, director of general maintenance
Jean Cocteau, guest
Charlotte Corday, assistant manager
Julio Cortázar, guest
Salvadore Dali, pest control
Madame Defarge, guest
Maya Deren, guest
Marguerite Duras, pastry chef
Gaston (rumored to be Robert Desnos), waiter
M. Godot, hotel manager
Dexter Gordon, guest
Jeanette, guest
Jorge, bellboy
Frida Kahlo, mental health counselor
Kiki, hotel restaurant hostess
Jerzy Kosiński, hotel librarian
Louis, house iguana
Joyce Mansour, night manager
Vladimir Mayakovsky, guest

Jeanne Moreau, guest
Thomas Merton, beekeeper
George Orwell, hair stylist
Pablo Picasso, hotel plumber
Georges Simenon, house detective
Susan Sontag, justice of the peace
Gertrude Stein, director of entertainment
Agnès Varda, guest
Remedios Varo, manager of food services
Saffron, hotel parrot

HOTEL MONTPARNASSE:
Letters to César Vallejo

*I'll die in Paris in a downpour
on a day I can already remember.*
--César Vallejo
tr. Kent Johnson

*The best thing is to be living,
and yet not living.*
–D. T. Suzuki

PREFACE

HOTEL MONTPARNASSE

September 26, 2020

Dear Mr. Bradley,

Greetings from the Hotel Montparnasse.

We hope the enclosed manuscript has found itself in the right hands. Our exacting house detective, Inspector Georges Simenon, located your most recent address. The one found amongst the enclosed papers—112 W. Merry Ave., Bowling Green, Ohio 43402—appears out of date. This Ohio address, scrawled across one of the documents, was located in the room once occupied by a certain guest who appears to have been an acquaintance of yours. This guest would be Monsieur César Abraham Vallejo.

While cleaning his room after his sudden (and most unfortunate) departure, the chambermaid found a pile of papers under his bed, bound with a piece of twine. As you may know, he departed the Hotel Montparnasse quite abruptly, leaving no forwarding address. The authorities have investigated his so-called *escape*, as a most annoying writer has called it, and they have found no trace of him as of this writing.

In his hurried departure, M. Vallejo seems to have forgotten that he owed the Hotel Montparnasse for various expenses. (He had an obsessive fondness for hot chocolate, with cayenne and a shot of brandy. He called it his "medicine." He would place three or four orders a night for his beloved "medicine.") Vices always come with a cost. His unpaid expenses total $3,190.99 (translated into your American currency).

If you happen to publish the enclosed manuscript, we trust you would promptly send us the proceeds to help reimburse Monsieur Vallejo's debts. The literary world lies beyond our terrain, but we understand that Vallejo's name possesses some cachet.

You'll notice many of the enclosed papers are signed "AC" and sometimes "Álvaro de Campos." We do not understand your connection with this M. de Campos. Perhaps you could kindly explain?

If you happen to know Monsieur Vallejo's current residence, please let us know at once.

Cordially yours,

Charlotte Corday
Assistant Manager
Hotel Montparnasse

P.S.
Jeanette instructed me to tell you: *Don't let the moon hibernate in your abdomen, or it will never leave.* She said you would understand.

CHAPTER ONE

 # HOTEL MONTPARNASSE

What, then, did the earth tell you, César, collapsing
on your coffin that day in Paris, talking to you with grunt
and crumble that go on all the time beneath any gravestone.

What, at that instant, did you give back to Peru, to the horse
trailing its reins on the cemetery gravel, to your feet, so cold
because someone pulled the warmth from your black socks.

Forgive me. I want to touch your face, wet and slippery
as it was on that day they dressed you in that cheap suit
creased with drowsy rage.

I want to know, César, and then I will leave you, amigo,
to the rest of your endless day—What time is it, now,
in your left middle finger? Right now, in your right orbit?
In the garlic clove someone slipped into your lightly
pulsing ~~tin~~ galactic coffin?

There's no hurry. Sometimes the voice is hard
to get started after it's rusted so long.

And the rain.

AC

HOTEL MONTPARNASSE

You checked into room number 39 because
that's the age of the worker who dug your grave.

And because you can't bear to tell the desk clerk
she needs a zinc bathtub of warm milk to soak
her tired feet--and tired back and skull—
for at least 39 minutes.

Relax, says the aloe plant in your window.
Nothing to fear, says the chipped radiator.
Says the newspaper's wilted corpse
on the faded floral carpet. Says the shirt
hugging the back of the chair
consoling the desk gone dizzy from staring
at the many coffee rings.

Nothing to be said, says that black pubic hair
clinging to the stiff, sallow lampshade.

A hotel room with closet, bed, sink, mirror,
because here it's harder for God
to pull you back to the morgue, back
to that dreamless hole in the ground.

Relax, says the mirror, *take off your clothes.*
And so you do. Falling back on the clean towel
you spread on the bed, your flesh tickled
by the nappy fabric.

Room 39, you say. The black hair still clinging
to the sullen lampshade.

Your friend,
Álvaro of the Campos

HOTEL MONTPARNASSE

This note was found in the restaurant this morning, César,
under a plate at the table where you usually sit. Gaston
has no idea who left it. I'm sure it's just an ignorant
prank.

Sincerely,
C. Corday

César Vallejo, you don't know me, but
I believe you might want to. Ignorance
works on the brain in Circles and Squares.

Don't wear your shoes to dinner tonight.
Keep your hands out of your pockets
at all times. An Autobiography needs

monstrous Monsters. Do exactly as I say.
Make sure you fly is half-open. Speaking
eliminates History, tropes, speaking.

Kiss Jeanette slowly on her neck. Order
Blood soup. And when the waiter asks you
what else you'd like this evening, tell him:

Think of the body as nothing but firewood.

[Unsigned]

 HOTEL MONTPARNASSE

But tell me, my friend, how did this happen?

How did you manage to leave your earth-tickling grave for a room in the Hotel Milky Insomnia?

With your prickly, swollen tongue?

With smoke rising from your hair?

With that train schedule inside your left shoe?

Did you take a drifting taxi?

Did the driver two-step you up the stairs of the hotel, waltz you into room 39?

Seat you at the desk and stick a pen in your hand?

So you could write:

> *The wind carries mountain crumbs, river saliva, bits of birds, exhausted travelers chewing on burnt leaves.*

Tell me, my friend. I won't tell.

Álvaro

HOTEL MONTPARNASSE

My Dear Monsieur Vallejo:

I couldn't help but notice your fine
feline, that most attractive sleek grey cat

lounging about your bed each time

I happen to go past your open door.
If I lent you my three-volume history

on the Punic Wars. With delicate watercolor

illustrations. Or perhaps you'd prefer
the personal copy of the *Kama Sutra*

signed by Napoleon's mistress.

You'd allow me a date with the grey?
One blissful night is all I request.

Tell me, does she like champagne?

Sake? Brandy? Would she prefer
glazed partridge or sweet cherry flambé?

I'll read her some Verlaine. Dante.

Sapho. And should she piddle on me
after dinner as we discuss if the Romans

really salted the fields of Carthage, well,

I would not mind, kind sir. Not at all.
Please grant me your considered

and compassionate consent.

Sincerely,
Charles Baudelaire

HOTEL MONTPARNASSE

Thou shalt not take the name of Mademoiselle Charlotte Corday in vain.

Thou shalt not give absinthe or aspirin to the houseplants.

Thou shalt not paint the windows aubergine or chartreuse. Saffron or crimson.

Thou shalt not take knife or tip of fountain pen to the thin membrane of the rain.

Thou shalt not mail a letter to an address beyond the hotel unless it has been approved by Mademoiselle Corday.

Thou shalt not spill or expel lubricant of any kind from the hotel roof.

Thou shalt not give Louis the house iguana spirits of any kind unless approved by Doctor Miguel Carablanca.

Thou shalt not sleep with your hotel room door locked (from the inside).

Thou shalt not take a bath with thy neighbor.

Thou shalt not covet thy neighbor's pillow or sleep mask. They are all *identical*.

Thou shalt not drop a book, no matter how much it
   displeases you (Monsieur Vallejo), down the laundry
   or trash chute.

Thou shalt not say *I shall die on a Thursday* any day of the week.

Thou shalt not set thy hair on fire, even if said hair *smells
   like cordwood*.

Thou shalt not leave a print of a bloody hand on the wine
   cellar wall.

Thou shalt be kind to Mademoiselle Charlotte Corday,
   even if weary, or sleepless, or sleepwalking, or speaking
   with a slightly injured tongue.

Thanking you in advance for your cooperation,
The Management

HOTEL MONTPARNASSE

You're sure you want to do this?
Dead Man's Bread can cause
dangerous, unpredictable effects.

You'll need a pomegranate
that's been frozen in a pond
for ninety days. Nine dead honeybees
(Don't tell Señor Merton).   Every third
page pulled from a copy
of *Paris Spleen*. A whisker
from a cat that has spent
eight of its nine lives. Twenty-six
drops of rain from a damaged
cloud. And the heat from
a vowel snagged in a spiderweb.

Place the loaf of bread outside
Baudelaire's door with a note
saying: *Not for Human Consumption*.

Remember. I never wrote this letter.

Your friend,
Frida K.

P.S.
Wash your trapezoid.
~~And deltoid~~.

HOTEL MONTPARNASSE

Date: September 10, 19 [Unreadable]
Time: 9:05 a.m.
Place: Northern Lights Dining Room

Charge: Creating and Maintaining a Public Nuisance and Disorderly Conduct

Complainant: Jerzy Kosiński, hotel librarian

Complainant's Statement:
I found him in the northwest corner of the library near the map cabinet doing something you don't ever do in a library.

Defendant: César Vallejo, library patron

Defendant's Statement:
Examine closely, ~~skull by skull,~~ the many brains in a hollyhock.

Judge Sontag's Statement:
With the powers invested in me by entities corporeal and non-corporeal, I hereby sentence César Abraham Vallejo to no less than six months janitorial duty in the Hotel Montparnasse Library, under the supervision of Monsieur Jerzy Kosiński.

M. Vallejo may not speak in the library, whether to inquire about the weather,

or a library patron's bodily temperature, or why
Trilce has been marked XXX, unless
it concerns a matter of life and death.
He may not pose questions that create
confusion about the fate of books,
or continents, or planetary exhalations.

Finally, he must wash himself
thoroughly each day, with industrial
strength cleanser.

Hearing adjourned.

Signed,
The Honorable Justice Sontag

N.B. I cannot be bribed, M. Vallejo,
with a box of macaroons. Not even
if they are made by the illustrious
Marguerite Duras. But—damn them—
those macaroons are dreadful tasty!

# HOTEL MONTPARNASSE

I was handed this today, César, on Rue Lautréamont, by a man with a long nose and a long red and black scarf wound round his neck. He wouldn't say his name.

Incinerate after reading.

Cheers,
Álvaro de Campos

When Poetry Is History's Fable

So Hitler came to live in a homeless shelter in Vienna, and he stole a battered bike. He rode it around the city, delivering bread. One day he brought a loaf of rye to a woman with poppies in her hair. He stammered, looked down, handed her the bread.

She smiled, smelled the loaf, and cursed him.

Who had urinated on her bread? She would call the police, the fire department, the president of the bakers' union. She would call the society for the protection and preservation of bread.

She slapped him. He stood there, unmoving.

And those roaches! Look at them scurrying
up her arm. Down her leg. Someone
hollowed out the loaf and put roaches in there.
What monster would do such a thing?

Hitler backed away, turned, slowly

made his way back to his bike. But he couldn't
get on it. The bike violently shook.
Threw him off again and again. He kicked
the bike. Shoved it behind a hedge.

It began to rain a cold, featureless rain.

From that day on, for the rest of his
Hitlerian life, Hitler gagged at the faintest
scent of bread. Fresh, stale, gray, chewed,
spit into a rubbish heap—any hint of bread
and Hitler fell to the ground and heaved.

Or so we want the poem to go.

HOTEL MONTPARNASSE

A swastika found spray-painted
on a pane in the greenhouse. Another
found scrawled in a stall in the men's
room off the lobby. Another
on the back alley door.

Even here, says Gaston.

Inspector Simenon has interviewed staff,
guests, even the rodents. No one knows
anything about anything. Our inspector
believes these instances are not a threat
just the doings of some fool
with an over-active pituitary.

Even here, says Alma.

Jean Cocteau gets hard looks
when he dines each night. Some say
he's been reading *Mein Kampf.* Writing
a play about a Hitler impersonator.

Even here, says Paul Celan.

Celan and Angel spread a thick
coat of whitewash over the swastika
found on the sun room ceiling.

Three days later, there it is
again, those long black tentacles
expanding
                twisting about.

AC

CHAPTER TWO

 HOTEL MONTPARNASSE

Dear César, you know what's coming.

The management, to whom I owe a certain
debt, has asked me to delicately inquire
about several calls you have made
recently to Room Service.

Last evening, for example. You
requested a woman named Jeanette.
Who must wear a black veil
and white gloves. To rub your body
with fresh straw, following your bath.

Also, they claim you demanded
the removal of your balcony
so that when you open the balcony
door and step out, only the damp air
remains there to support you.

They take great pleasure, they say,
in granting your wishes. However—
and there always lurks a *never*
within each *however*—beginning Saturday
you must report for the first shift
at the hotel restaurant as—
I don't know the French for it
so I will use the crude term—a busboy.

They hope you will approve
of this arrangement. Otherwise
and I quote the hotel doctor:

> *We are most afraid Monsieur Vallejo*
> *will begin to fade from view. An arm.*
> *Part of a shoulder. A piece at a time*
>
> *making it difficult for others*
> *to know if Vallejo is here, with us,*
> *or somewhere else. Or perhaps both*
> *at the same time.*

Jeanette could explain all this
much better than I could, I'm sure.

As ever,
Álvaro

P.S.
The house doc, a certain Miguel
Carablanca, was a horse doctor
they say, somewhere in Spain.
He claims he can speak Inuit
but not a word of Spanish. *The mere*
touch of Spanish against my skin,
he says, *and I break out in hives.*

HOTEL MONTPARNASSE

I can smell sulfur from a distant comet
hissing in your hair. Clay threading
through your shirt. Cuffs damp

as the salamander on the basement
floor, not far from the furnace.
Your breath giving off the scent

of after dinner mints. Those dark
chocolate mints Jeanne Moreau loves
to give to each new arrival

on their first day at the hotel. This
morning Gaston spilled some coffee
on your shirt sleeve.   Its acidity seeping

into yours. Your eyes deeper, darker.
Such things happen just before
they begin to happen. The nervous

clamor in the brass bell beside
your bed, just before your cold
hand quells the tremor in the bell.

A de C

HOTEL MONTPARNASSE

*Don't forget what your hat and shoes
will look like when you are nowhere
to be found.*

You copied these words into your notebook.
To not forget them.   And yet

we forget, in all our parts, to be as human
as a Venus fly trap, with its sharp teeth.
As human as the deeper silence in the lower
spine. In the nipple's quiet intent.

You shaved today with the radio on. News
of a suicided angel in Zanzibar and then
that perfume ad with the phony Chinese song
that makes your ankle in its motile core feel more,
yes, proto-human.

Even those cockroaches in the wall, those dreaded
all-too-dental entities, they, too, ur-human,
pulsing to the chinoiserie music.

So after you shaved, César, the towel rasping
against your damp flesh, as if I couldn't hear you,
as if I would forget: Your voice, soggy
on the foggy mirror intoning: *Caught
once more in the groinal sway.*

And so you are.
               And so are we all.

Faithfully yours,
Álvaro of the Campos

HOTEL MONTPARNASSE

Yeah, Jean Cocteau and I
were once friends. Didn't I already
tell you this story? We were working
in a warehouse full of coffins.

He sat down during a break
and I could see he wasn't wearing
any underwear. Only his lederhosen.
And by his look I could tell
he saw I wasn't wearing
any underwear. Only lederhosen.

He reported me to the foreman
who told me this was disrespectful
to the dead who would soon be
inhabiting those coffins.
He would have to fire me.

I wanted to say, *But Cocteau, he
isn't wearing any underwear!*
Only my tongue felt like someone
had stitched it to the bottom of my mouth.

Later, I heard about an infestation
of moths flying around the warehouse.
The toxin on their wings, if inhaled,
could sicken or kill.

When I saw Cocteau a month or two
later, in his lederhosen, sipping absinthe
at a café, I thanked him for getting me fired.

> *You human turd*, he said. *You could
> have gotten me fired and saved me
> from that place. But poets.
> Poets are such great cowards.*

AC

HOTEL MONTPARNASSE

Would I like you to shave my legs?

Would my legs like to be shaven
by your hand?

Would I like your hand on the razor
that shaves the hair on my legs?

Would I?

I would like nothing more than to float

       from eyelid

             to island

       to eyelid.

That open.
       That close.

Your body a wave
       with a hole in your center
             a tunnel through the stars.

Your
Jeanette

HOTEL MONTPARNASSE

I've left the items you requested,
César, with Jorge, the bellboy. *Visitors,*
he said, *can no longer leave
the lobby. Security,* he noted, as if that word
explained what cannot be explained.

After I pressed into his hand
a wad of crumpled bills, he smiled,
happy to slip you the package.
The manager, he confided,
is a genuine ostrich turd.

Here's what you should receive:

>Six white candles
>A package of eucalyptus incense
>Tweezers
>A bag of cotton balls
>An enema bag
>*The Egyptian Book of the Dead*
>A black garter belt
>Three black candles
>Seven jalapeños

I charged all the items,
as instructed, to the Peruvian
Embassy. They must think
quite highly of you, amigo.

Salud,
Álvaro

P.S.
I couldn't find a bottle of milk
from an albino llama, or the dung
of an Egyptian alligator.
~~Or Jeanette's death certificate.~~

HOTEL MONTPARNASSE

Well, there's not a lot known
about Jeanette. Like all the guests
at the hotel, she rarely speaks
about her past. But Alma, she who knows
all, filled me in as she was cleaning
the lobby this morning.

Jeanette and her husband
were shopkeepers for one of those
places where you could buy
a box of cheap cigars, a pricey bottle
of wine, a dirty magazine, a box
of rat poison, a lightbulb, birdseed,
and on some Saturdays, if you were lucky,
a glass eye. André, her husband,
liked to listen to opera. Though
if you asked him, he'd say he hated it.

What else. Oh, Jeanette died
in a car crash, her body pulled out
of the wreck. That explains the scar
on her neck. She likes to sit
on her balcony, most afternoons,
read *The Song of Solomon*
and smoke clove cigarettes.

She faints, claims Alma, *at the sight
of a glass of burgundy. That's just*

how it is here, she added, and then went back to her dusting.

Unofficially,
Inspector Simenon

HOTEL MONTPARNASSE

You tell the story again, and I pretend
I've never heard it. To hear your voice
go soft as an old shoe left in the rain.

Alma was so sure someone
had marked you, so sure
she wouldn't dare enter your
room, until you promised
to search in the mirror for it: *666.*

It was greenish, Alma remembered
from her dream, speaking with her back
to you. The numbers somehow reminded her
of that two-faced god she saw
on a coin in the museum.

*Which also had one of those
you know, clay grave figures
with the man and the woman
joined below by this large*,
her neck shuddered, *coil of clay*.
And then she stopped turning
her ring round and round.

So there you were, the white
of your ass in the mirror
as you looked for that tattoo,
666, coiled on your backside.

Nada, you said. *No mark
of the beast.* But she wasn't
convinced. Left your bed unmade,
and that night peered through your keyhole
to see if you were a demon.

What did she see? A skeleton,
lying on his back, skeleton hands
under his skull. Ready to float
wherever his bones wanted him to go.

Julio

HOTEL MONTPARNASSE

Before there was red, César,
there was only black and white.
White and black and all
the shadows in between.

One night someone knocked over
a pot of boiling water. The burning
water fell on a baby's arm,
face, belly, foot. Red eyes,
red teeth, red song shooting
from the mouth.

*Exterminate, so that you yourself
will not be exterminated*, said the voice
on the radio.

Because a red face
will say the same thing
as raw filet mignon. Because
if you do not see red, you will
see only black and white, and all
the shadows in between.

Who else but,
Leonora

HOTEL MONTPARNASSE

Angel was polishing the leaves of the rubber plant in the lobby.
Alma was painting her toenails, listening to Billie Holiday.
Saffron, in her brass cage, shouted *Mon Dieu*, just before it
    happened.
Jeanette, in the reading room, studied the hotel's wine list.
You were in the bathtub reciting from *The Egyptian Book of the
    Dead.*
You chanted: *I lie down dead. I am born daily. I lie down in death.
I am born, I become new, I renew my youth every day.*

The bomb was sent in a package addressed to César Vallejo.
The return address said it was from the Marquis de Sade Society.
The delivery man was never employed by the parcel company.
The police want to know everyone you know, César.
The police want to know why you have a scar on your left leg.
The police want to know why your middle name is Abraham.
Why is your middle name Abraham?

Two men in the dining room were arguing over the veal.
One said it came from Paraguay. The other, Uruguay.
Gaston thought they were from Argentina.
Kiki said they smelled like wet paint and had Martian accents.
The bomb thought the veal looked like a leather wallet.
The bomb sent it back to the kitchen.

Jeanette recalls seeing you in the lobby smoking a cigar.
Jeanette recalls you lighting your cigar as the bomb went off.
The police want to know why there's a powder burn on your
    sleeve.

A powder burn the shape of Argentina.
The hotel is now serving drinks in the bar free of charge.

The manager says these things happen everywhere.
The police are taking your clothes to the lab.
Alma says she sprinkled oregano and sage over your hair.
Jeanette is in the chapel smoking a clove cigarette.
The hotel lawyer says you have no reason to worry.
She says he has a cousin who knows the chief inspector.
Jorge, the bellboy, is coming to your door with a bottle of
    champagne.
He says he does not know who ordered it.
Just before the bomb went off Jeanette says she heard you say:
I shall not enter into the place of destruction, I shall not
perish, I shall not know decay.

[Unsigned]

CHAPTER THREE

HOTEL MONTPARNASSE

Dear, Dearest César,

That welt on your spine. It will and it won't. So beautiful.

Swallowing a 60-watt bulb. Your eyes, they'll burn. Day and night.

To be cured in a situation such as yours. Much needs to be practiced.

My mother stood on a chair. Saying: *Not talking is pretty much talking.* But try. Not to talk. For at least 28 days.

Try this: Go up to the roof of the hotel one night. Naked. Lie there with legs spread apart. Arms apart from the body.

Then roll the tip of your tongue. Under your tongue. Repeat these words: *This is perhaps the last day of my life.*

Many times. More than you can say.

Say it. As no historian could.
The way Hamlet meets Hamlet in Act V of *Hamlet*.

Then come see me. Do. And I will give you a kidney stone. To clutch and to carry.

Which will much improve. Most things.

Everyone's doctor,
Miguel (Carablanca)

HOTEL MONTPARNASSE

Regarding that rumor of a diagram of a bomb found in
your room, Monsieur Vallejo:

Nineteen vowels cocooned with five carnivorous teeth.
An elephant named Illustrious disappearing a tack and an ax.
When my father couldn't fix the bullet hole in the turtle shell.
Each time you made me press myself against the
    pulmonary valve.

Back when I collected chicken-shack tin, found the
    arsenic rosary.
Suckle upon this, she said, a small snail shell on her tongue.
Electricity scattered by dragging a radio on a leash made
    of lemon peels.
To expel fox blood. Artichoke dung. Dried rhino heart.

Back when we salted the snow with radiator ash.
Back when you spoke epiglottal Latin.
Back when a stick of bacon could be forgiven as a trick of
    dynamite.
Back when every story began: *Reading the future in your flesh.*

When a sanitary rain smeared your face into lateral thorns.
Dear father pouring his milky novenas down the bullet hole.
Mama preaching congealed Sunday morning egg yolk.
Tell me again how you secreted a starfish.

Back when you electrocuted the dogwood.
Back when you worked nights as a bolt cutter.
Below the zebra's part-battery, part-narcoleptic liver.
The exfoliated diagram of the moon under your eyelid.

[Unsigned]

HOTEL MONTPARNASSE

When asked why he made origami bombs, day after day,
he said: *Drink a shot glass of liquified starlight each*

morning. But why would anyone circle the heart, circle

the heart with a mile of red thread? Ambient rain. Parked
car sinking into drunken soil. Words melting in the lingual

heat. *Go groom your tongue*, she said, packing the pulsating

light in a crate, to ship to a buyer in Panama. In the cedar
   chest:
an ivory comb with five missing teeth. Ampersand
   from a movie

marque. Burnt shoelace no one will discuss. *The Book
   of Ecclesiastes*

As Inscribed on a Preserved Swan Tongue embedded
   in the sternum.
Blind Willie Johnson in the chinaberry tree. But why
   would anyone

circle the heart, circle the heart with an orbit of red thread?
   For hours

he comforted the apple tree with a warm blanket
   and a burnt apple.
The mouth knows. Words melting in the lingual heat.

The one and only,
Jean Cocteau

HOTEL MONTPARNASSE

Because now they ~~fornicate~~ violate your mail,
César. Because if you sleep, when you sleep,
your shoes beneath your pillow.
Because laudanum is a stopwatch
wrapped in gauze.

I write you this morning in pencil
on a napkin, as you can see.
To startle you in the way Alma's
lipsticked lips almost did. When she tried
to make you feel less woozy.

*Anywhere. Anywhere out of this
world.* Those bawdy words
your wrote on your mirror.

That set loose a frantic animal
under your skin. What the bomb did
to your face. You forgot
to mention in your last letter.

Because now they torture your mail.
Because if you sleep, when you sleep,
a stopwatch beneath your pillow.

Because laudanum is a starfish
wrapped in gauze.

Ever vigilant,
Djuna

HOTEL MONTPARNASSE

There was a line for tickets, but
only three customers could approach
the window at a time. I stayed
away, waiting.

When I finally made it there, facing
the barred window and the grim clerk
I couldn't find the money
you gave me. Instead, I gave him
an airmail envelope
with your words scrawled
on the back:

> *And female is the soul*
> *of the absent. And female*
> *is my soul.*

He read it, blinked a few times.
Looked up at me. Shoved
the envelope at me, slicing
his tender finger. He cursed.

Instead of a ticket, he pushed
a band aid at me. Still wrapped
in the prophylactic wrapper.

I laughed, struggling to open
the damn thing. I finally managed
to unwrap it and slid the naked bandaid
back under the bars. He grabbed it.

I want to buy him a scarlet parakeet
with a scalding, barbed-wire song.
Leave it in his kitchen.
To go off whenever he comes near.

Campos de Álvaro

HOTEL MONTPARNASSE

I came across a faded book of Chinese
poetry tossed into a garbage can. These
words made me think of you, César:

> *And a fierce anger burns within me:*
> *It's thinking of how I've wasted my time*
> *That makes this fury tear my heart.*

I copied it and asked Gaston
to stuff it inside your flounder.
I hope you won't eat the anger
in those words.

As I copied them, a tiny spider—
almost too small to see—fell
from the tip of my pen.

What does this mean, César? Please.
Tell me what all this could mean.

Jeanette

HOTEL MONTPARNASSE

You left the hotel *without official leave*
according to your police file, César.
Wandering about barefoot, saying, *My blood.*
Has anyone seen those thirty-nine
syllables of blood?

Beneath a seat in a lecture
hall, you found your raincoat
sprinkled with olive oil and garlic.
A meal for a goat? You shook
it out, showering oil on a man
with a braided beard.

He stood, breathing in your face
his testicular, amphibian sigh.
A turtle gasping on a reef
for some Brahms, some Coltrane.

You were next seen
in a pharmacy on Rue Voltaire.
Salt my tongue, you ordered a woman
with a scar in the corner of her mouth.

Outside, you bowed to a pharaoh
who had just escaped his sarcophagus.
He did not bow back.

You stumbled over a black cat
you said you knew was
Charlotte Corday.

You collapsed onto a faded
red sofa in the alley across
from a small TV, waking to hear
a reporter say, *I'm just happy
the monster has no pulse.*

AC

HOTEL MONTPARNASSE

Compadre,
I heard from Jeanette that Joyce Mansour, just a few doors down from yours, can't be found. She was last seen on Thursday, washing her hair with snail shells and champagne. They found the snail shells in her sink and the empty champagne bottle, but no Joyce. Perhaps the hotel can use this text, below, for a flyer?

Álvaro

For Joyce Mansour, Lost in Cairo

Every third window. You said
I could find you in Cairo behind
every third window. A tobacco pipe
filled with red sand. A cat with a bandaged
tail. A lizard that speaks in a tongue
heard only with a damp wrist.

You carry a violin case, but you won't
tell me what's inside. I write
on your wrist: *In Cairo, the moon
possesses glass teeth*. You laugh.
An onion rolls across the street.
Who placed that bandage
at the base of my spine
while I was asleep?

Behind every third window

I find twenty-three grains of sand.
You tell me to gather them
in an envelope. Mail them back
to you. But you left no address
on my wrist. Only the drawing
of an ibis. Much too hungry.

HOTEL MONTPARNASSE

Monsieur V,
Copied from Inspector Simenon's ever-expanding
archives. Something for your poetry, no?

Destroy after reading.

Cheers,
Orwellian George

Report of an article of clothing (unclear—
a scarf? A handkerchief?) flying off the body
of a guest while eating mushroom soup.

Report a of a small fire in a guest's
wastebasket. The origin of the fire a copy
of Baudelaire's *Paris Spleen*.

Report of a swarm of gold teeth (bees?)
swirling around the hat of Madame Defarge.

A report of someone sawing a leg,
a wooden leg, at 3:03 in the morning.

Report of a baby crying in the laundry
chute, heard by several guests.

Report of a ram wandering the third
floor corridor, chewing the carpet
(it does appear to have been chewed.)

Report of a herd of flamingoes seen
wandering the sub-basement.

Report of the sound of chiseling
late Sunday night, as if someone is tunneling
through the hotel foundation.

Report of ground sleeping pills
stirred into the mushroom soup.

HOTEL MONTPARNASSE

César,
Gertrude Stein read this last night at her latest so-called "Dangerous Soiree." She dedicated it to you in hopes you'll feel better soon. As she says, *Sooner than better.*

AC

Let the millionaire's hat roll down the hill.
Let the hill roll after the millionaire, rolling after the hat.
Let the hat nap while it rolls, the hill a conspiracy of
    calcified clouds.
The hill where I nap, where I told the hill:
I am ambidextrous, but I am not yet Dexter or Philbert.
Let Northumberland roll, roll down the reeling hill, the hill
far from an ambidextrous hat.
Let the hat speak for all those who roll down horizontal hills,
roll down vertical faces, roll whatever cannot stroll.
Let the hill tell the ailing millionaire, with marzipan and
    flan, *Roll,*
roll after your collarbone, before your collarbone rolls.
Let the roundabout hat tell no one where it rolls, the hat
    without
head or home, but somehow always finds itself a rolling
    hailstone
in the hills of Northumberland.
The hat and the hill and the rolling bread roller and the
    napping
and the salivating spoon, after the last act, after the fact of
    the hat.

Let the rolling end here, says the hat, near the head without
    a hill,
near an elbow that appears almost flat.
Let the heavenly hill millionaire tell us why there's a cloud
on the head of the hill worth millions of hats.
Let the cloud tell the hill why the millionaire keeps rolling,
all the teeth strolling, why the rain keeps calling the hat
a rolling along randy, rainy day fact.
O let the sea take the hill and the heart-rattling hat, and
    let the millionaire
go on rolling, long after the hill curls up into a masticated hat.

CHAPTER FOUR

HOTEL MONTPARNASSE

It's the solstice. Cigarette butts floating in the toilet. Jeanette calls. She's starting to lose her hair, she says. Wants to know why your room never has an ashtray. She complains to Alma who complains to Kiki, the restaurant hostess. Someone knocks on your door. The hotel detective, Monsieur Simenon, carries off your bedtable lamp. Alma, scrubbing your door, asks: *Do you ever think about ants having, you know, sex?*

The solstice. There's a rip in the armpit of your favorite shirt. Strands of light can be stored, you read, in an ice cube. Jeanette calls. She's going to shave her head at noon. *Would you hate me*, she asks, *if I wore that scent called Avarice?* A knock at the door. *Your lamp is working much better now, sir*, says Guillaume, the electrician who fears lightning. You tip him generously, though your lamp had worked just fine.

Yes, the solstice. The hotel is serving cantaloupe à la mode for lunch. Thomas Merton translated your sock with a hole in the toe into a poem. A strand of light is trapped inside the ant in your teacup. Jeanette calls. *Should I rub aftershave on my head?* Alma vacuums your carpet. You see a tattoo near her ankle: *666*. She's in your closet a long time, the door locked. You peer through the keyhole. An eye peers back.

For it's the solstice. You take a hot bath, reading *Nemo: Adventures in Slumberland*. The phone rings. A woman wants to know if you'd like to buy a grave plot. Jeanette is at the door in her new wig. *How do you like me as a blonde? At night I'm going to be a red-head.* A taxi pulls up in front

of the hotel. The driver claims you called for the cab.
A strand of light lays its eggs in the iris on your dresser.

Álvaro de Campos

HOTEL MONTPARNASSE

Due to the sudden vowel shortage:
No chatting over the rutabaga soup.
No bathing before 6 a.m. or after 7 p.m.
No room service after midnight.

No snake cleansing in the greenhouse.
No leaning against the grandfather clock.
No painting the kitchen Venice green.
No chewing on the sun room wallpaper.

Due to the severity of the vowel shortage:
No radios or umbrellas will be repaired.
No Our Lady of Garlic dinner rolls.
No surgical demonstrations in the wine cellar.

No swearing at the staff during breakfast.
No tracing of the moon's runes on the walls.
No recording of yawns, Monsieur Vallejo.
No exemptions until further notification.

Thanking you for your cooperation,
The Management

HOTEL MONTPARNASSE

That photo you sent, César, I find it rather
disturbing. In the sun room of the hotel,
there's you, Madame Defarge, Doc Miguel
(Carablanca), leaning over to examine

a photograph. But where you stand
there's only an outline of your body.
A black hole. A door frame in the shape
of César Vallejo. I can see soot and stars

in that doorway, a dog with a bomb
strapped to its back, that psychic from Barcelona,
Don Carlos, at the table, waving his arms,
telling all: *Come closer, come closer.*

*I find it comforting to think about
Arctic creatures*, Mlle. Djuna Barnes
tells the physic. That's when
the itinerant photographer shoots the photo.

*At night, salt contains the taste
of starlight*, the photographers confides
on his way out. You shake his hand
and then he leaves with your image

locked in his leather portmanteau.
On the back of your photo, stamped
in black ink: *Arthur Rimbaud, Explorer
of the Celestial Realms of Photography.*

Cordially,
Maya

HOTEL MONTPARNASSE

So sorry you had to wake this morning

and lie there in bed with those tiny
green shoots rising through your wrist.

Pull them out! Now! I heard you shout

at Doctor Miguel, at his leather gloves,
at his epilator, at his telling you

Just watch my pocket watch

in hopes of hypnotizing your panic
into a state of sleepy boredom.

So sorry, say the tiny green threads

pushing through your flesh.
Though you know they are not

sorry. No one is ever sorry,

or guilty, or sleepily bored,
or yells *Infuse me with green, green!*

enough.

Your upstairs friend,
Julio

HOTEL MONTPARNASSE

In Minsk, mercury leaks from the leg of a ladder.
In Lima, a man rubs axolotl oil on his swollen tongue.
In Beirut, a school bus is swallowed by a dragonfly.

This morning, you ate grapefruit and a breaded sparrow.
I devoured a toasted bagel and the brain of a woodchuck.

In Seattle, a mine shaft opened in a coyote's ankle.
In Galway, coiled lightning was found inside a turtle.
In Kyoto, a whiskey glass said: *I need teeth made of peat.*

You chew the spleen of a buffalo for dinner, César.
I masticate the shank of a radioactive reindeer.

[Unsigned]

P.S.
Wash your collarbone
with *Moonlight Sonata.*

HOTEL MONTPARNASSE

That smoky scent on your flesh—you've burned another library copy of *Paris Spleen*.

Last night I dreamed you hammered your father into the earth. With each blow, your body letting out a small sigh.

The electricity in your toes, César, the same as that found
    in any tuber,
any turbulent vowel. Any pomegranate pierced with nails.

How deep a condemned angel must burrow into this flesh.

If I step on a worm, I am a star with no core, no history, only beginning and unbending, endlessly unending.

Right now, tell me again: *The center of this universe is here—Jeanette's purple comb*

resting in a basket
on the back of a toilet.

AC

HOTEL MONTPARNASSE

*Last night, I was in a tunnel, right
next a stalled train. The engineer, his face
smeared with oil, pushed the train
engine as if he could make it move.
And the train inched forward! I woke
sweating, my entire body shuddering.*

*Everyone here, when they first
arrive, gets a whirring headache.
Later, they can't remember
anything. But me, I remember
everything.*

*I was on the hotel roof one day
taking in the laundry, and the wind
lifted my skirt. Rubbed my groin.
I said to the wind,* Go jump off
this building, you damn fool! *And the fool did exactly that.*

*You should try sprinkling sage
over your sheets. You'll feel
better if you move your bed
and sleep polar north. Then
you won't wake up with the taste
of a dead bird in your mouth.*

*

That's my lecture today
from Alma, the source of all
wisdom. Please don't share this
with anyone, César. I don't
want to embarrass her.

Your one-floor-above friend,
Julio

HOTEL MONTPARNASSE

Check your door, César, several times
a night. Make sure the deadbolt knows
it's a dead bolt. Wipe the mirror with circular
motions, always clockwise. Wash your underwear
and socks in the bathroom sink with a plum
and then wash the plum. Pick up the phone
at 3:33. Listen. But say nothing. Say
Thirty-three thirty-three times a day.
Make sure your voice is ready.

Sit quietly on your bed every twenty-one
minutes. Focus on the shadow of your head
there on the carpet. Focus on the center
of the center of the center.

When the closet door slowly opens, don't
act surprised. Take a sip of water, swallow,
reach over, turn the lamp on and then off.
When you do shout, start low, your voice
barely rising above the carpet at first.

Then leap to your highest pitch, your
shout blurring his features. The tiny
bones in his inner ear aching, branches
too heavy with spring snow.

He'll fall to his knees, one hand
on his throat. His larynx vibrating
from the impact of your shout.

This is important. Tell him to go downstairs, boil some milk. Add three ice cubes and a shot of apricot brandy. Sip it. You should too.

I don't believe that intruder will ever bother you again.

Remedios

HOTEL MONTPARNASSE

One day you find under an iron tree a heel of bread
embedded with bits of mica and metal. You bite

into it, chew. You feel the shards lightly gouge

your mouth, then gather in the heart's dim
chambers. One day someone with thick fingers

combing through loosened earth uncovers a heart-

shaped lump of metal. Then under an iron tree
delicate strokes hammer the heart, hammer

the heart into a swarm of drowsy arrowheads.

Julio

P.S.
Wash your vowels
with zebra sleep.

 ## HOTEL MONTPARNASSE

The Paris light, César, eating
you through on the one side,
eating you through on the other.

And in the middle, you

huddled in bed, hands
cupped around a termite's
unsung wing. Eaten through.

[Unsigned]

P.S. Eaten through.

CHAPTER FIVE

HOTEL MONTPARNASSE

Say something about the arsonist who set aflame
the sign proclaiming *Hotel Montparnasse*.

Say something about the pocket watch, how it conducts
the beating of the heart, though the heart never listens.

Say something about Jeanette before Jeanette says
she never met César Vallejo in the wine cellar where
he asked her if she wanted to hear a cricket symphony.

Say something about the fear of sleep, how sleep
unravels the lines that moor the Hotel Montparnasse
to curb and cobblestone.

Say something about Tu Fu and Ikkyū and the ocean
with its belly full of moon. The moon with its belly
full of fluttering moon fish.

Say something about the morning when no one
in the hotel could get out of bed, how Doc Miguel
had to come around and give each guest
an injection of red chile and polka.

Say something, if you can, about the hammering
each night in the basement, the chiseling through
the foundation wall, the buckets of chalky masonry
dumped each morning along the back alley.

Say something about the glint of light from a gold tooth, how the light from this tooth makes anyone it touches yawn and forget

the sayer and the said.

AC

HOTEL MONTPARNASSE

I know what happened, César. Julio told me
last night in the lounge, while Dexter Gordon
played "Sleepwalking to the Sleep Factory."

Genevieve, the manager's wife, let me see
the charges filed against you:

> *Irresponsible use of poetic license
> in a public space. Inciting
> a hotel guest to imbibe dangerous
> reading materials. Damage to
> the hotel's foundational structure.*

Madame Defarge testified:

> *He destabilized a guest with his
> malicious and dangerous shout.*

The man's face began to blister and peel,
she said. Doctor Miguel revived him
with massive doses of Pachelbel's Canon.

If you had shouted one more time
at him, the victim would have suffered
molecular deconstruction, claimed the doc.

So you are under house arrest. Confined
to your room for an unspecified

duration. No guests. No telephone
calls. No more midnight massages
with Jeanette.

All charges will be dropped when
you sign the vow of silence.

Jeanette will be bringing you
a copy of the vow and a cup
of Russian thistle tea
(and a shot of vodka).

Your friend and supervisor,
Jerzy

HOTEL MONTPARNASSE

Your voice, César, spreads a light pink-
and-red vegetable mist. Through which ostrich
morphemes meander.

This is what happens each time you tell me:

> *When you make love on a cat-hair-covered sofa,*
> *you make love to all the syllables*
> *in your grandmother's marrow.*

Your voice a vow, woven with willow and lilac,
silk and seared air, soaked in kerosene.

The rasp of earth-stutter rising up, rising
through your shoes, through your homesick

skeleton, igniting the little hum
at the end of your cigarette.

Álvaro

HOTEL MONTPARNASSE

I'm traveling faster now. That's the last
thing Ray Carver said before leaving
his body. Is that how it was for you, César,
leaving Santiago de Chuco for Paris, leaving
Paris for Russia, Russia for Paris, leaving
Paris for Spain, Spain for Paris? Then leaving
your grave for the Hotel Montparnasse.

Traveling faster, always faster.

Last night I saw a film you would like,
my friend. Perhaps you saw it one Saturday
night in the lounge, with the young couple
in the back playing Russian roulette, until
the revolver fired: a red flag. And they collapsed
in laughter. Madame Defarge hissing: *Why don't
you two use a real revolver for a change!*

In the film, two angels travel to West
Berlin and listen to the whispering
going on inside the skulls of humans.
You know: *How can I ever tell Zsuzsanna
I used her toothbrush to scrub the toilet?*

One of the angels falls in love with a circus
acrobat. And becomes human. Such a strange
thing. Why a spirit would ever want
to dwell again in flesh. In heart rage

and lung burn. In tooth throb and raving
tongue. Traveling ever faster.

AC

P.S.
Don't worry, César. I won't tell Jeanette
what you did with her toothbrush last night.
The red one with the gold sparkles.

HOTEL MONTPARNASSE

You've shaved, César, the first time in several days.
Bits of beard stick to the white enamel basin.

Julio, one floor above, strums that wretched guitar
he made with a cigar box and rubber bands.

Kiki stays in her room with the door locked.
She says you know why.

Jeanette sits in a large leather chair in the lobby
reading *The Story of O*. Whenever Mr. Simenon nears
she closes the book and smiles.

Angel has polished your black leather shoes
and left them at your door. Inside the left shoe
someone left a note: *Wash your face with volcanic ash.*

Julio is now chanting: *Sleepwalking to the sleep factory.*
Dexter Gordon yells, *Julio, insert your sleep-loving
head in the toilet!*

I won't ask why you stare at the water pitcher.
Where the blades of a blue windmill on a hill
refuse to turn. Over and over.

Frida K.

HOTEL MONTPARNASSE

The wind lives in a vase in the yellow house
on the hill, so I'm told. I tell you I've never been
inside that house on the hill where the wind raves.
When someone stole into the yellow house, I was asleep
on side of the hill, the wind pulling at my clothes.

Why would I steal that homely vase from the house
on the hill, smash it on a rock, and bid the wind
obey my command? Why, the wind would grow mad,
flail about, fling you far from the hill where
you accused me of consorting with the wind.

Then I'd have to confess: *It's true, the wind forced
its way down your throat until you choked.
Then flung you far from the broken vase, while
on the hill I slept the most delicious sleep.*

[Unsigned]

 HOTEL MONTPARNASSE

And so this guy says to his friend
who happens to be a wheelbarrow,

*Tell me, amigo. Don't you get tired
of being a wheelbarrow?*

And his friend says: *Hey, I'm lucky.
I got to be a wheelbarrow!*

*

Something to make you laugh,
César. Or maybe groan.

Yours,
Jeanette

HOTEL MONTPARNASSE

Here's my list of *Impossible Things*, César. Eager to read yours.

Remedios

Selling a black robe—more
a constellation of moth holes—
and a bucket of coal, each piece
the exact size of a starless hole.

*

Parting the babble with your
bare hands, as if it's nothing
but a curtain of beaded rain.

*

Cleansing your lover's body
with warm milk, boiled ash,
ground heron eggshell, before
and after making love.

*

Eating a copy of *Trilce*
each morning, in order
not to eat the wing of a moth.

*

Finding you stuck
to the ceiling by your back.
We wave a spatula
pray to the household ants.

HOTEL MONTPARNASSE

Two pedestrians, in long black coats, waiting
for the bus. About twenty feet away, near
a telephone pole, an angel—tall, thin and a bit
glassy-skinned—nods once, nods twice.

At that moment, the two pedestrians vanish.
The friends of the missing know the absent ones
are dead. The absent ones, however, don't know.
In fact, they believe they're very much alive.

*Transference of matter through somatic time
and space.* That's what the angel would call it
if you asked. And when the transfer fails,
which it does on occasion: *Sometimes the brain
does not wish to be beaten into a soufflé.*

*Where are their bodies? How did they perish
so suddenly?* the friends of the missing wonder.
But the missing two, now in another state, find jobs
and lovers, find sturdy beds and sturdy desks.

The angel thinks it funny, how much the two
like their shiny, wooden desks. How they stroke
the vibrant wood. Wipe away the dust. Place an ear
to the grain and listen, listen to the wood whirl.

The angel, for some reason, cannot laugh,
so it rocks slightly forward and backward.
And then once again, forward, backward,
there, near the telephone pole by the bus stop.

[Unsigned]

P.S. Divine capture?

HOTEL MONTPARNASSE

I know you'll hate this idea, César, but
hear me out. All the management requires
is for you lie for a while in an open coffin,

eyes closed, hands at your side.
Not visibly breathing, if possible.
You'll be in the sun room, surrounded

by white candles and lilacs, there
in your gleaming white coffin, while
Madame Defarge holds her séance

for Joyce Mansour. I can hear her
fog-horn voice calling out, *Joyce
Mansour, wherever you are, come,*

*come to us now. Loiter and linger
with us. Speak through me. We beseech
thee, Joyce Mansour.* And that's it.

Nap for a bit. Then, when everyone
has left, you sit up, stretch our your arms,
climb out of your white chariot,

and you'll be allowed to speak
again. (Though not too loudly,
please.) Then they will tear up your vow

of silence. That's not such a bad
deal, is it, César? Tell them,
I've never felt so refreshed.

Then saunter off to your room.

Xoxo,
Jeanette

CHAPTER SIX

 ## HOTEL MONTPARNASSE

They're afraid of you, César, afraid
of the axolotls that escape
your mouth. You ask so much

of us. Perhaps too much. You want
us to remember what hides inside
lake, rock, organ. Inside blood
walls. Those slinky shapes
that want so much
to make us sigh, to drive
every turn of the brain.

Until
this body bends
to each shift in the wind.
As we watch. As we pass
ourselves by.

Let's take a stroll tonight
in the Serenity Garden. You
with your Peruvian tungsten
cane. Me with my vertiginous
hummingbird feather scarf.

Both of us
blindfolded. Arm
in arm.

Always,
Jeanette

HOTEL MONTPARNASSE

This was found on the floor, under your temporary coffin after the séance. Madame Defarge claims it's a message from Joyce Mansour. Of course.

You had nothing to do with this, César. Right?

Jeanette

Angel with otter whiskers.
Angel with a fish for a brain.
Angel with aquamarine eyes.
Angel that wears 4-D glasses.

Angel that walks through chairs.
Angel with a sack of angel dung.
Angel that swallowed a revolver.
Angel with a birchwood snuffbox.

Angel with a scar on the lower lip.
Angel that sleeps in a cheese sandwich.
Angel that turns vodka back into potatoes.
Angel that listens to John Coltrane in the abattoir.

Angel with six round windows in the side of its head.
Angel with six fingers on one hand and nine on the other.
Angel that reads *Paris Spleen* in a tree made of barbed wire.
Angel that goes by the name Ahava, Jabbok, Arnon, Euphrates.

Angel that saith: *A great eyelid beats the air over the turning earth.*

HOTEL MONTPARNASSE

I know what you're doing, friend.
Reading Ecclesiastes. In bed. Naked.
Punishing yourself. Because

that guest in the restaurant last night
reading your poem that begins *For several days,*
I have felt an exuberant, political need to love.
While eating the celebrated rabbit stew

he began to choke on a small bone
and had to be taken away. I've heard
he coughed up the bone, turned,
and died on the way to the hospital.

His last words, said a medic: *To help*
the killer kill, a terrible thing.

Don't be so hard on César, César.
He could have been reading anything
while he ate the stew. And the same fate
would have felled him.

Tell me, do you like rum raison crème brulee?
I asked Marguerite to make this tonight
just for you and Jeanette.

Your barbarous barber friend,
Orwellian George

P.S.
Stop by for a free shave.
This time the straight razor
will be sharper than sharp.

HOTEL MONTPARNASSE

Alma told me—forgive her, friend—
you've been copying something
in your notebook. Over and over.

These lines by a soldier
whose fiancé had been slain
in the war. Such terrible, lovely lines.

> *Once I loved my country*
> *because of the birds and butterflies.*
> *Because there were days of escaping*
> *from school. But now I love my country*
> *because in each handful of soil*
> *you are there, my beloved.*

Please, be kind to Alma tomorrow
morning. She will bring you
the red lacquered tray
with a basket of freshly baked
croissants. A vase of pink
hollyhocks. Pot of green tea.

For you, she'll say
about the croissants. The tea.
Your ravenous grief.

What she won't say:

~~My dearest fool.~~
Wash the heart's root
with the silence
clinging to the root.

Onward,
Julio

HOTEL MONTPARNASSE

Because the stars, so far below, so far above the roof of the skull.

Because the tongue, wobbling, chittering, rasping.

Because the thirst, in the middle of the tongue.

Because the spine, wobbling, chittering, rasping.

Because the thirst, in the root of the tongue.

Because the stars, so far above, so far below the roof of the skull.

~~Because,~~
Álvaro of the Campos of the Álvaro

P.S.
Sometimes called *divine capture*.

HOTEL MONTPARNASSE

A revolver with three bullets.
Underneath your boxer shorts
in the top drawer of your bureau.

How did you ever imagine Alma
would not discover it?
A revolver with three bullets

she buried at the bottom of the large
clay pot of oregano on your windowsill.
Oregano that Alma waters

each Sunday morning. Knowing
the roots will grab and hold
the revolver and its three bullets.

How could the gun and bullets
not succumb—as do we all—
to her constant care.

The three bullets giving birth
to a plague of snails.
Now they wander floor and wall

of each room in the hotel, looking,
always looking for home: the empty
chambers of a sweaty revolver.

Julio

HOTEL MONTPARNASSE

Dear Mademoiselle Corday,
a green bird. Not a bird that is green,
except for the red beak. Not a green bird
with a slash of red down its back.
No, a fever-green bird

for my dear friend, César Vallejo,
pacing his pallid room. I ask this knowing
too well his blind passion, the panicked
pulse of his brain.

I request, just the same,
your kind permission for the gift
of one too-green bird, kept always
in a sturdy cage, for César, who
possesses such a deep, inevitable
need. How he hungers for that green—fragrant
and wild and almost fit to eat—inhabiting
vibratory feathers and flesh.

In return for this permission,
I would be pleased to teach you
on the night of each full moon
on the open balcony, outside
your room, how to speak
in the language of birds, and say:

> *Green, how I want you, green.*
> *Green feathers. Green flesh.*

Of course, this may be too much
to ask. Yet would it not
be in the interest of the hotel
to calm the spirit tormenting
César?

You know best.

Respectfully yours,
Jeanette

 # HOTEL MONTPARNASSE

Last night, when all the lights
in the hotel went out, you were boiling

a salamander egg, orange peels,
a black hat, a tuning fork, and

a piece of the banister railing.
Some salt stuck to your palm.

Remember?

When the lights came back on
you found her hand lying upon

your notebook—reading, through
her palm, through the cover, each
terrible word.

Remember?

And then you accused her. Jeanette.
Of spying. Plagiarizing you.

Remember?

She turned. Left. You did not move.

Everything in the room, in the hotel
going through you
going through.

Remember?

Press your right hand to your forehead
for three minutes and twenty-nine seconds
exactly. And you will remember.

Remedios

HOTEL MONTPARNASSE

Rain, tapping on my shoulder
all night. I know what it wants
me, wants you to say:

> *Each droplet*
> *of rain—a tiny zebra*
> *with platypus feet.*

Ever,
Leonora

P.S.
Wash wash wash
your tabula rasa.

HOTEL MONTPARNASSE

Written in soap on the mirror in Vallejo's room:

Paul Celan does not like to be touched.
Remedios Varo does not like talking turnips.
Frida Kahlo will not eat uncooked termites.
Robert Desnos does not like to wear a tether.

Leonora Carrington does not like to be tickled.
Jerzy Kosiński does not like to cut his toenails.
Kiki will not go near a jar of pickled tonsils.
Federico García Lorca is allergic to pasta à la Franco.

Charlotte Corday does not like a wet wig.
Apollinaire does not like to ride in a blimp.
Mayakovsky does not like to be truncated.
Julio Cortázar does not like a wet matchstick.

Gertrude Stein does not like to be called Twinkle Toes.
Joyce Mansour cannot tolerate the sound of a tuning fork.
Pablo Picasso will not dine near Charles Baudelaire.
César Vallejo does not like giving birth to César Vallejo.

[Unsigned]

CHAPTER SEVEN

HOTEL MONTPARNASSE

No, César, I don't think you should
tell anyone. It's bad enough

they found the taxi at the bottom
of the Seine, the engine frozen. Worse

if you explain how you and Artaud
slipped out of the hotel, drunk

on Irish whiskey, and recited
Siberian shaman owl chants

as the taxi plunged
into the arms of the Seine.

There is a reason the shoe's tongue
doesn't tell the sole how far

they are from the moon.
No, I don't believe the mayor

of Paris will grant you political
and poetical asylum.

Your next appointment with me
is on Monday, 8:45 a.m. Please

wear socks. And this time let's
make sure your finger doesn't stray

into the electrical outlet.
Your worldly and spiritual adviser,

Frida K.

HOTEL MONTPARNASSE

Later, after you were questioned
concerning the poetry books
in the hotel library

how nearly all the books
are missing page 64.
Only page 64.

After your room was scoured
and they found this poem
in a shoe, torn from a book:

> *In this living world*
> *the body I give up and burn*
> *would be wretched*
> *if I thought of myself as*
> *anything but firewood.*

Which, I'm pleased to say,
bears the number 49 (not 64)
in the upper right corner.

After they interrogated you
for three hours in the wine cellar
you unzipped and zipped

your fly several times, I'm told.
A sign of deference and respect
argued your lawyer, Gertrude Stein.

No wonder you stole
into the kitchen late last night
and left all the onions soaking

in badger blood.
I tell you I would have
done the very same.

Always,
Orwellian George

HOTEL MONTPARNASSE

Because the eye doesn't want to hear
about the erotic nature of geometry.
Because the cat in the window lives
in the path along your optic
nerve. Along with everything else.

So what, you say. *So what.*

The lobby cat, Brutus, anchored
to his carapace. Until the moment
he floats out of its hold.

So what, he says. *So what.*

That is to say, I would like
to tell each organ inside Brutus:

> *You work so hard,*
> *my little friend. For what.*
> *For what. Now is the time*
> *to let go. Just let go.*

Even if it is true.
    Even if it is not.

Until the moment it is.

Julio

HOTEL MONTPARNASSE

This time we were in a diner
that looked like an aluminum cigar.
I bought a pack of Marlboros
for those captives in the back
of the truck across the street. But
I gave it to you instead.

Our bus was taking us somewhere
into the mountains. You crawled
under your seat, looking
for a hat you said you lost
on a bus in Peru.

The mountains breathed
a greenish mist that reminded you
of a distant relative. An old
woman near us asked if you
would kiss her. You remembered
her white hair, pinned just so
into braids, from an old photo.

You kissed her forehead
in front of a storefront
with a sign that read: *Home
Valve Repair.* A ladder
beneath the *e* in *Home*
placed there by someone
who left for lunch.

That old lady studied your hand
César, for a long time. You must
remember this. She rubbed
your knuckles and said: *Querido*.
That's all she would say.

Álvaro

HOTEL MONTPARNASSE

Your ravenous heartbeat. They have masked it, César.

Baffled the sound. Beneath geese flight, filing cabinets,
dirigible. Discolored wood, glass wheel, bog, turbine, goggles.
Rising river, car horn, glockenspiel, bridge cable, index cards.

Dust motes.

Then dropping from a great height an iron apostrophe
on someone who cannot be clearly seen.
And therefore matters as much as mulch.

Erased. Your heartbeat, Cesar.

Until I thought you were Dr. Miguel's
human skeleton, Señor Duende, lying next to me, there
in my moonlit bed, the gravid dark breathing
all around.

And you wait, and you wait for me to be so stupid
as to close my eyes.

Jeanette

HOTEL MONTPARNASSE

At 4 a.m., I see you in the middle
of your black raincoat. On a street
that smells of Turkish tobacco.
Your heart a fox in a cigar box.

You chew on a coffee bean
a long time, then cough. Pointing
to a black ant, its abdomen glistening
in the rain, you say, *Be ready, in case
of a sudden opening in the magnetic field.*

At 4 a.m., a policeman asks: *And what
brings you connards here at this hour?*
Turning your head away, you mutter:
*It's always the anvil, s'il vous plait,
that breaks the hammer.*

At 4 a.m. a calico cat watches you
with the eyes of an infected doctor.

You tell the cat, *Before you sleep,
my friend, forget all you know.
Then, only then, let sleep erase you.*

Your de Campos camerado,
Álvaro

HOTEL MONTPARNASSE

Something for your digging, César.

A. Artaud

In Other Violence Today

I dig a hole in the below. Therefore. The hole digs a hole
in me. Therefore. I carry a piece of dirt between cheek and gum.
The dirt carrying a piece of flesh and foamy wish. Therefore.

I cannot be seen from my right side. Your left. I bump
into buildings on my left. Your right. Therefore.
I address you with my whole hole and my whole non-hole.

Therefore. I call you out as Dirt Seed Carrier, Flinger of
    Filleted
Dirt, Dirtaceous in Mouth, Mouth Surrounding Many
    and Much
Fibrously Mouthed Dirt. Therefore. You do not often address

either portion of me. Please. Do not mail me clam shells,
    pasta
shells, bullet shells, skulls stolen from pyramidal foundations.
Therefore. The rain will not rain unknown heart particles upon

the brain. You will eventually come to some kind of evidentiary
end. Therefore. However soon soon is. Hereafter. I leave you
to ponder the all in all. The hole in the below. You as you are.

Therefore. Wheresoever I am.

HOTEL MONTPARNASSE

A votive candle on the radio
in your room, burning.
While you're down below

tunneling.

A narrow opening
in the foundation, to escape
a larger, more confining

opening.

A burglar who steals
only himself from
himself. A liquid verb

tunneling.

Living, and yet not living.
Dying, yet not dying.
That note you forgot before

tunneling.

Forgot to leave
by the radio
with the white candle

burning.

Small participles
of skin and sleep
all around you

floating

in the air, while you—
with spoon and tin
cup—always

tunneling.

[Unsigned]

HOTEL MONTPARNASSE

Don't tell, César
anyone

      about that violet light

from your navel
leaking still.

Yours,
Doc Miguel

P.S.
If you walk in a circle
make sure your tongue
keeps moving
in a circle.

HOTEL MONTPARNASSE

Thou shalt walk, César Vallejo,
in large, unattended spaces.

Thou shalt hear what joy
reverberates through
the mouse's spine, what lingers
in the snake's vertebrae.

Thou shalt rain salt
on thy head and thy bread
place on a flat stone.

Thou shalt sleep
with a Friday and know
what the flea knows
and what the flea does not.

Thou shalt comingle
with tibia and clavicle, even
with the prostate
and not fear.

Thou shalt go listening
to the quiet that gathers
in gutter, cistern, elbow.
The unspoken speaking
unquiet human vowels.

Thou shalt pass, César Vallejo,
through a distant boulder
and come out the other side

to walk in unattended circles.

AC

NOTES

Parsing this rather odd manuscript, I notice various—to use the polite term—borrowings. Here are my findings.

Inspector G. Simenon

Page 26, in *"Don't forget what your hat and shoes,"* the opening three lines are from a poem by Bob Perelman.

Page 37, in "Before there was red, César": *"Exterminate, so that you yourself will not be exterminated"* was stated by Hitler.

Page 38, in "Angel was polishing the leaves" the lines beginning *"I shall not enter / into the place of destruction"* come from *The Egyptian Book of the Dead*, as translated by E. A. Wallis Budge.

Page 48, in "Because they now ~~fornicate~~ violate your mail" *"Anywhere out of this world"* is from Charles Baudelaire's *Paris Spleen,* as translated by Louise Varèse.

Page 49, in "There was a line for tickets, but," the lines *"And female is the soul of the absent. / And female is my soul"* come from poem IX, in Vallejo's *Trilce*, as translated by David Smith.

Page 51, in "I came across a faded book," the lines beginning *"And a fierce anger burns within me"* come from Yuan Chi's poem "Regret," translated by Arthur Waley.

Page 98, in "This was found on the floor," the line "*A great eye beats the air over the turning earth*" comes from *The Thief of Talant*, Pierre Reverdy, tr. Ian Seed. The names of the angels—Ahava, Jabbok, Arnon, Euphrates—come from rivers mentioned in the Bible.

Page 99, in "I know what you're doing, friend," the lines beginning "*For several days*" and" *to help the killer kill*" are from a poem by Vallejo, translated by José Rubia Barcia and Clayton Eshleman.

Page 101, in "Alma told me—forgive her, friend—," the lines beginning "*Once I loved my country*" come from Gloria Emerson's *Winners and Losers*.

Page 115, in "Later, after you were questioned," the poem that begins "*In this living world*" was composed by Ryonen. Translator unknown.

Page 121, in "At 4 a.m., I see you in the middle," the phrase "*It's always the anvil that breaks the hammer*" was stated by George Orwell.

APPENDIX

October 21, 2020

Dear Reader,

A second mailing of documents arrived on October 4, this time with no introductory letter. The envelope, postmarked in Paris, had no return address, only an "A.C." in the top left corner. Indicating that the sender was my dear friend Álvaro de Campos?

The ten documents, held together by a rusty paper clip, contained the following texts, in the order that they appear here. With the various introductions and signees (or lack thereof).

I must say that I've heard the persistent rumors that this entire enterprise is an elaborate, or should I say devious, plot to embarrass me. To suggest I am somehow involved in this rather dubious enterprise. Though why someone should feel such an urge to entangle me, I do not know. Certainly I have literary enemies, as do all poets. It's part of the "po biz" experience. But why go to all this trouble to prove I'm a fool? I'll gladly shout it, in any town square, from any empty plinth, on any day, fair or foul.

I've also heard the names of poets—two in particular— who could be playing the role of this Álvaro de Campos, one of the heteronyms of the astounding Portuguese poet Fernando Pessoa. Both of these potential pranksters are poets I knew in a writing program decades ago. I've contacted both of them. One told me, *Damn, I wish I had thought of that!* The other has yet to bother to reply. But again, I wonder why anyone would go to such trouble. And why, in their attempt to involve me, dishonor Pessoa and Vallejo? Or does the writer believe that they are honoring these poets with this curious project?

At any rate, here is the second installment, which I have added as an Appendix. I assume (and hope!) this will be the last of the "Letters to Vallejo." I leave it to the reader to make of them what they will.

Respectfully,
John Bradley

P.S.
Opening the envelope, a scrap of paper fell out, bearing these words, written in pencil: *Read this if you can. Read this if you can't.*

 HOTEL MONTPARNASSE

Jeanette sent me this last entry, César, from your last journal.

(Or is it hers?)

AC

    And the people made of ash would eat
only ants made of wood, and the people

made of wood would eat only lizards
made with lightning, and the people

made of lightning would eat only
the flesh of the people made of ash.

HOTEL MONTPARNASSE

Found inside the rooftop pigeon coop, with a razor
blade taped to the bottom of the second page.

Yours in perpetual vigilance,
Inspector Simenon

For C.V.

It cuts. It cuts and it cuts and it cuts.
It knows who to cut, where to cut, knows
the streets that crease, streets that cut and shear.

You stumble, falter, slide sideways and down
on the serrated street, where a round-cheeked woman
bites her serrated lip, down and around, through
the streets, where the blade cuts.

Do not stumble. Do not halt, falter, fall
in the streets. Streets with sharp, pointed
corners. Streets, scarred and scared,
scared and scarred from the cutting, the constant
cutting in the streets.

How does it feel to be cut, sliced
in the street? How does it feel in the street
to be cut? No one. No one dares ask.
If they ask, never answer. Answer
by surrendering no answer.

He hemorrhaged, there, in the street,
and he could not at that moment even spell
hemorrhage, or *street*, or *cut*. Spell *here
where the street hemorrhages.*

I was cut, long ago, scraped and cut
from my mother, where it no longer
hurts, so I could be here, near the street.

I was cut, there, where it does not matter
anymore, where the flesh, gone useless
from so many cuts, only throbs because
it no longer hurts.

Yes, they cut and cut, and, cutting through
the cut, cut through the street, through
the purple tissue underlying each street.

Cutting, until the cut, unable to stop, gets up,
sways, there, in the tilting street, wobbling
about, until there is nothing around, nothing
within, nothing but cut.

Down the tottering street, the cut
stumbles, looks for someone not tottering,
someone to grab, plant a kiss on, leave
there on the neck a cut, so the cut
would not hurt alone.

Until everyone was cut, everyone
throbbed, and no one noticed

if someone, there, in the street,
in the gutter, bore the cut.

Yes, even now, it cuts. It cuts
and it cuts and it cuts.
Even when you say you can't hear
it, can't bear the sound,
it cuts. It cuts and it cuts and

we cut.

[Unsigned, except for a small "Z," with a horizontal bar through the center, in the bottom right corner (Ƶ).]

HOTEL MONTPARNASSE

Frida claims she found this in a small suitcase in her storage unit in the basement. She says the suitcase could be Jeanette's. I can affirm that this document was typed on Jeanette's typewriter. Though, of course, we don't know whose hands were doing the typing.

Faithfully,
Inspector S

The Art of Invisibility

Every year I swear I'll learn how to translate those frost-written runes on my window.

*

Glacial starlight, she told me, *it's the only food my stomach can tolerate.*

*

While you were busy napping, someone filled your coffin with tarnished spoons.

*

The moon pleases everyone; I please only the moon.

*

Why is it so much easier to forgive falling snow rather

than endless tundra?

*

The last book you will ever read: *The Art of Invisibility*—
upon the touch of the reader's eye, the world dissolves.

[Unsigned]

HOTEL MONTPARNASSE

Inside a coyote's stomach, I can attest I once found:
one horned toad, armadillo armor, nine bumblebees,
one rattlesnake, three centipedes, rope, tire
rubber, one harness buckle, five birds' eggs, bits of
honeycomb, and assorted pebbles.

Inside the stomach of Vallejo, they shall find: a library
copy of *Paris Spleen*, part of a leather glove, iron
shavings, a bar of soap, one small bottle of Delirium
perfume, part of a poster for a flea circus, a harness
buckle, honeycomb, rope, a vial of rain, and assorted
pebbles.

As ever,
Doc Miguel (Carablanca)

P.S.
Wash the hands with timothy, sea salt,
mercury. Wash the hands with sassafras,
ground bone, arsenic. Wash the hands with ginger
root, clay, fire. Wash the hands with *followed by,
blurred words, swirling around, long before.*

HOTEL MONTPARNASSE

This so-called "Interview with César Vallejo's Death Mask" came into my possession from "Doctor" Miguel Carablanca. He said he found it in the laundry room. Alma says she found it in the attic, under a brick wrapped in burlap. Gaston says he found it in Jeanette's hatbox. Jeanette claims she found it in, get this, Doc Miguel's room, underneath a jar of Amazonian wombats, afloat in formaldehyde.

Zoot alors, says Saffron. *I don't know if we should frame it or burn it*, says Doc Miguel. Therefore, I conclude: Author unknown. Or as César would say, *Not presently restricted to any particular bodily form.*

Tirelessly,
Inspector Simenon

Into and Out of This World: An Interview with César Vallejo's Death Mask

Q. Is it true you worked in the back of a print shop repairing oboes?
A. Listen, if it weren't for my intestines, I wouldn't be here.

Q. What is mesmerism and why do you keep rubbing a spoon around your navel?
A. On the radio, the Atlantic is saying, *I want to be inside you, male person, female person.*

Q. What did the inspector pull out of your mouth?
A. When I first drew a woman inside a cow, my mother killed it.

Q. How do you prefer to cleanse the brain?
A. Dust from Neptune can be found in one out of eight babies.

Q. Who read your tea leaves on that street where you carried a box of books on your head in the rain?
A. The mail slot on the fifth floor keeps panting.

Q. Is it true you fit a kitchen into your comb into your typewriter into your coffin?
A. You move your tongue a certain way and all the lights in the world go out.

Q. Narrate your passport photograph using ash and a bit of spittle.
A. An elephant being called an ant being called a bathtub made of lead.

Q. But that's not what your bodyguard told us.
A. To the streetsweeper, everything looks like a poem.

Q. Didn't the inspector's wife say she never met you?
A. One night we live long, one night nobody can see the line from louse to movie house, from philtrum to film studies, from myopia to cinematopia.

Q. Didn't you once tell [*inaudible*] that memory lives in the belly of a termite?
A. There are portals all around us that lead into and out of this world.

Q. Because you consider this an interrogation, not a fugue for two voices?
A. I hate luck, I hate dead batteries, I hate the body at a séance in Norway swirling round and round.

Q. Weren't you sighted at the Café du Monde in bathrobe and fuzzy slippers and hairnet?
A. Nobody born, nobody unborn.

Q. What did Carl Jung tell you on January 19?
A. A bowl of somatic cabbage soup, not far from a dog's nonverbal region.

Q. A cough, you once said, can alter history. Please explain, using red and green circles and squares.
A. Rake, each morning, the sand in your bed each night.

Q. Are you, in any way, attached to the [inaudible] moon with unseen wire?
A. I am a little bit inside you, male person, female person.

Q. But the inspector . . .
A. I never look at a cat or dog and not see bacteria in outer space.

Q. But the inspector . . .
A. I've always had a fear of gauze and the like. Gauze stuffed in a red chile slipped into a bamboo flute hidden in a chimney flue.

Q. I was once asked by a Trappist monk, *What is the color of Vallejo's soul?*
A. Go ahead and step on your mother's grave, your feet tangled in tin sardines.

Q. Tell us more about your spiritual practice of gargling with gasoline.
A. There are portals all around that lead into and out of this world.

HOTEL MONTPARNASSE

Found tucked into a copy of *Trilce* at the Shakespeare and Company Bookstore, in Paris. The Mushinsha / Grossman edition, 1973 (with a mustard cover and faded light green spine), translated by David Smith.

Written inside the front cover, in black ink: *Non-edible.*

Your ~~non-edible~~ friend,
Álvaro de C.

We Do Not Mourn You, César Vallejo

How to undo all this clamor?
I ask you, César, as you eat your daily
bowl of shredded fact. Another draft
of "Black Stone on a White Stone." This one
where you die sprawled on the roof
of a hotel, in the rain district of Paris.

Unknown all that is known,
you say unto the bowl. To the dusty
granules. Dispersing each seed into
your innermost ear, where God
may be hiding. For particles of God
live in tree salt. Horse harness.
Arithmetic. Ear ache. *Too
visible to be seen,* you say.

But do not sever the line,
you mutter, knowing how blood
bends and thrums in the folds
of the brain, sings in the unending
spinal vowel, feathering now
into the here, so near
the almost always too far.

I do not mourn you, César Vallejo,
you insist, addressing perhaps
the long wire running from the back
of your head into the wall socket
and back. Fetal electricity
forcing you to speak into
and out of your carapace.
Your thorax. Your dura mater.
Your César. And, of course,
your inevitable, ~~your illustrious~~
Vallejo.

[Unsigned]

HOTEL MONTPARNASSE

I remember. I can't remember.

Bury me, you said, *with a hammer
and a chisel. Blind hammer.
Babylonian chisel. Bury me*

*with an angry beehive
that my tongue might be
stung awake and asleep.
Asleep and awake
at the same time.*

*Bury me in the hill that floats
above the almond tree.
Bury me in a droplet of rain.
Bury me in the intestine
of a worker termite.*

Bury me, you said,
*until no word loiters
to curse or bless.*

The wind rushing through
your enormous forehead.

I can't remember. I remember.

Your faithful beekeeper,
Thomas Merton

P.S.
I placed a copy of *Trilce*
and *Paris Spleen* in
your coffin, César.
Just in case.

HOTEL MONTPARNASSE

This text, as well as the next, were allegedly found by Gaston Bachelard, director of mail services, in Vallejo's dusty mailbox in the hotel. Not sure if Monsieur Bachelard actually found them, or perhaps placed the documents there himself. Or someone else placed them there.

Sigh. One can only report the known.

Inspector Simenon

A cough comes to the door and knocks.
A handkerchief is folded with the blade of a knife.
A woman raises her voice in the back room.
Two hands slide beneath an onion.

Can human fingers grow inside a melon?
Can bruised flesh make the sky go purple?
Where does the carpenter go when the nail sinks in?
Where did Mary Magdalene plant the *Book of Charred
    Roots*?

Any world, you said so gently, *can be removed.*
A cup of brown eyes could be a currency.
The earth possesses no tongue.
The earth possesses constellations of tongues.

Seal the entrance to the body's soil,
you once told me, César, and the doorframe will crack
without a sound.

Once, on a bridge, I opened my fly
and watered the long concrete grave below.
Should I water your grave, amigo, balanced
upon one leg, in order to balance the world?

Inside your coffin, a book thumps shut.

 HOTEL MONTPARNASSE

Do not disturb the back door. Those
who hide inside the shifting grain. Do not disturb
the sparrows on the back porch. Those
who hide inside the shifting sparrows.

In this way the lungs sustain the birds.
In this way the birds sustain the sky.

*

The earth cannot be closed, and so birds open
their lungs. Making it hard not to breathe
bird, dust, star field, night, tea kettle, leather, iron,
bits of dry dung. No wonder Chuang Tzu
tells of a man who sealed all the holes
in his body except for one
at the base of the spine.

Only a door, say the birds.
Only a door, says the sky.

*

My head is a ball of clay. My head is wood.
My head shaggy with bark. If I plant a crow
in my head, I see only the feathery, dank light.

How a face forms through the articulation of bone
pulled near the earth under the weight of desire.

My head a bulb. My tuberous head.

Below, says the earth.
Above, says the sky.

HOTEL MONTPARNASSE

And then, with my fingernail
I scraped the lichen from the stone.
I stripped the blur from the corrupted

letters. And then, no longer bound, words
began to blink and flutter. From this
flickering swirl I could hear:

> *Let my vital force now attain the immortal air.*
> *Now let this body be reduced to ash.*
> *Remember—remember all that has been done.*
> *Remember—remember all that has been done.*

And then, the light calmed. The letters
settled once more into place—still, clear,
dead. And then I read:

      CESAR VALLEJO
      1892-1938

[Unsigned]

NOTES

(As prepared by the indefatigable Inspector G. Simenon)

p. 133, "Jeanette sent me this" makes reference to a "last journal" kept by Vallejo. No such journal has been found.

p. 134, The poem "For C.V.," which was signed "Z" has spawned rumors about the author. Some speculate Z is an obscure Italian poet named Roberto Zingarello.

p. 140, "Into and Out of This World: An Interview with César Vallejo's Death Mask": Yes, there is a death mask of Vallejo, but it has given no known interviews as of this writing.

p. 152, In "And then, with my fingernail," the four lines beginning with "*Let my vital force now attain the immortal air*" are from the *Isa Upanishad*. Vallejo's birth and death dates, 1892-1938, are indeed accurate. More than that, I cannot say.

NB: My Dear César Vallejo, you must burn this manuscript, if you really wish to escape the dreaded hotel, burn it and ingest the ash.

About the Author

JOHN BRADLEY was born in Brooklyn, New York, and grew up in Framingham, Massachusetts; Lincoln and Omaha, Nebraska; Massapequa and Lynbrook, New York; and Wayzata, Minnesota. His first book, *Love-in-Idleness: The Poetry of Robert Zingarello*, won the Washington Prize, in 1989, and a second edition, expanded and revised, was published by Word Works. Besides writing poetry, he is also fond of composing aphorisms; his aphorisms appear in the anthologies *Short Flights* and *Short Circuits*. He is the recipient of two National Endowment for the Arts Fellowships, a Pushcart Prize, and a grant from the Illinois Arts Council. He has been reviewing poetry books for *Rain Taxi* for many years and currently is an assistant editor for *Cider Press Review*. He lives in DeKalb, Illinois, with his wife, Jana, and their cats, Kiki and Zuzu.

For the full Dos Madres Press catalog:
www.dosmadres.com

www.ingramcontent.com/pod-product-compliance
Lightning Source LLC
Chambersburg PA
CBHW021425070526
44577CB00001B/65